Mastering Microsoft PowerPoint: From Beginner to Pro with Skipton Tech

Preface

Welcome to "Mastering Microsoft PowerPoint: From Beginner to Pro with Skipton Tech." This book is designed to be a comprehensive guide to mastering PowerPoint, the powerful presentation software that has become a staple in businesses and classrooms around the world. Whether you are a complete novice looking to create your first slide or a seasoned user aiming to streamline your presentations, this book will provide you with the tools and knowledge you need to succeed.

Overview of the Book's Goals and Structure

The goal of this book is simple: to make you proficient in using Microsoft PowerPoint, regardless of your starting skill level. We aim to equip you with both the foundational skills needed to build and design compelling presentations and the advanced techniques that can help you work more efficiently and effectively.

The book is structured to gradually build your skills, starting with the basics and progressing to more advanced topics. Each chapter is designed to focus on specific aspects of PowerPoint, ensuring a logical flow that makes it easy to follow:

1. **Getting Started with PowerPoint**: Learn the basics, including how to navigate the interface and create simple presentations.
2. **Building Your First Presentation**: Dive into adding and managing content like text, images, and graphics.
3. **Design and Layout**: Focus on making your presentations visually appealing using themes, templates, and design tools.
4. **Multimedia and Animation**: Add life to your presentations with multimedia elements and animations.
5. **Advanced Tools and Techniques**: Master advanced functionalities like linking, embedding, and collaborating.

6. **Efficiency and Expert Tips**: Discover shortcuts and expert tips that save time and enhance your presentations.

7. **Preparing for Presentation Day**: Get ready to deliver your presentation confidently with tips on reviewing, practising, and presenting.

How to Use This Book to Maximise Learning

To get the most out of this book, we recommend starting at the beginning and working through the chapters in order. Each chapter builds on the last, with practical examples and case studies that allow you to apply what you've learned in real-world scenarios.

At the end of each chapter, exercises and quizzes will help reinforce your knowledge and ensure you have mastered the key concepts before moving on. Additionally, take advantage of the resources listed in the appendix to further your learning and stay updated on the latest PowerPoint features and best practices.

Whether you're preparing for a critical business presentation or looking to improve your classroom lectures, "Mastering Microsoft PowerPoint" is your go-to resource for becoming a PowerPoint expert. We are excited to help you on this journey to creating engaging, effective, and professional presentations with PowerPoint.

Chapter 1: Getting Started with PowerPoint

Introduction to PowerPoint

Microsoft PowerPoint is a powerful presentation software that is part of the Microsoft Office suite. It is used worldwide by professionals, educators, students, and anyone needing to create polished, professional presentations. PowerPoint allows users to present information visually, combining text, graphics, animation, and multimedia to produce compelling slides that can communicate ideas effectively.

PowerPoint presentations are composed of slides, which are individual units of the presentation. Each slide can contain a variety of content, including text, images, charts, and videos, making it a versatile tool for both simple presentations and complex multimedia displays.

Installing PowerPoint

Before you can start creating presentations, you need to install PowerPoint on your computer. PowerPoint is available on multiple platforms, including Windows, Mac, and through the Office 365 subscription service, which also offers access to online versions. Here's how you can install PowerPoint:

1. **Windows**:
   - Purchase Microsoft Office from the official Microsoft website or obtain a licence through your organisation.
   - Download the Office setup from your Microsoft account page.
   - Run the installer and select PowerPoint (along with any other Office apps you require).
   - Follow the on-screen instructions to complete the installation.

2. **Mac**:
   - Buy Microsoft Office from the Microsoft website or get a licence from your institution.
   - Download the Office setup from your Microsoft account page.
   - Open the downloaded file and follow the prompts to drag the Microsoft Office folder to your Applications folder.
   - The installation will integrate PowerPoint into your Applications.

3. **Office 365 Subscription**:
   - Subscribe to Office 365 online.

- Log in to your Microsoft account and select to install the Office suite.
- Follow the installation prompts on your screen.

After installing, open PowerPoint by clicking its icon in your applications list. The first time you open PowerPoint, you might be prompted to activate your software with your Microsoft account.

Navigating the Interface

Once you have PowerPoint open, you'll be greeted by the user interface which is intuitive and user-friendly. Here are the main components:

- **Ribbon**: The ribbon is located at the top of the window and contains all the tools and commands distributed across various tabs like Home, Insert, Design, etc.
- **Slide Pane**: This area displays the current slide. You can click on elements within the slide to edit them.
- **Thumbnail Pane**: On the left side, you'll see a vertical column showing thumbnails of all your slides. Clicking a thumbnail will bring that slide into view in the Slide Pane.
- **Notes Area**: Below the Slide Pane is a section where you can add notes for each slide. These are not visible to the audience during the presentation but can be a handy reminder for the presenter.

Creating Your First Presentation

To start creating your first presentation:
1. **Open PowerPoint** and select 'New Presentation'.
2. Choose a template or select a blank presentation to start from scratch.
3. Click on the 'Click to add title' and 'Click to add subtitle' boxes to add your first slide's content.
4. Use the ribbon to add new slides, choosing the appropriate layouts for your content.

Adding your first few slides will help you get comfortable with the basics of inserting text, choosing designs, and understanding the layout options. As you progress through the book, you'll learn how to enhance your presentations with more advanced features.

This chapter sets the foundation for your PowerPoint journey, starting from installation to creating your first simple presentation. As you become familiar with the PowerPoint environment and start experimenting with adding slides and content, you'll be ready to explore deeper functionalities discussed in the upcoming chapters.

Chapter 2: Building Your First Presentation

Working with Slides

One of the first things you'll want to master in PowerPoint is managing your slides effectively. Whether you're adding, deleting, or rearranging them, understanding these basics is key to building a smooth presentation.

1. **Adding Slides**: To add a new slide, go to the "Home" tab and click on the "New Slide" button. You'll see a drop-down menu with different slide layouts such as Title Slide, Title and Content, Section Header, etc. Choose the layout that best suits the content you plan to add. Alternatively, you can simply press "Ctrl+M" on your keyboard to quickly insert a new slide with the same layout as the currently selected slide.

2. **Deleting Slides**: If you need to remove a slide, click on its thumbnail in the left sidebar to select it, then press the "Delete" key. Make sure you're deleting the right slide, as this can't be undone unless you quickly press "Ctrl+Z" to undo.

3. **Rearranging Slides**: To change the order of your slides, click and hold on a slide thumbnail in the left sidebar and drag it to its new position. This is useful when you want to better organise your presentation's flow.

4. **Duplicating Slides**: Sometimes, you might want to use a similar layout or content on another slide. Instead of recreating it from scratch, right-click on the slide thumbnail, and select "Duplicate Slide". This will create an exact copy right after the original slide.

Each of these actions helps you craft the structure of your presentation, setting a solid foundation for adding content. By mastering how to manage your slides, you're well on your way to creating a compelling PowerPoint presentation that flows logically and engages your audience.

Text and Bullet Points

Text is a fundamental element of any presentation, helping to convey your message clearly and effectively. Here's how to add and format text in PowerPoint:

1. **Adding Text Boxes**: To add a text box, go to the "Insert" tab and click on "Text Box". Then, click

anywhere on the slide to place the text box and start typing your content.

2. **Formatting Text**: To format the text, select it by clicking and dragging over the text you want to change. Then, use the "Home" tab options to:
   - **Change the Font Style and Size**: Select a font and size that make your text clear and easy to read. Larger fonts work well for titles, while smaller fonts are suitable for body text.
   - **Adjust the Alignment**: You can align text left, right, centre, or justify it depending on how you want it to appear on the slide.
   - **Add Colour**: Choose a text colour that contrasts well with the background for better visibility.
   - **Apply Bold, Italic, or Underline**: These options can help emphasise important points.

3. **Using Bullet Points**: To organise information clearly, use bullet points. Click on the "Bullets" icon in the "Paragraph" group under the "Home" tab to start a bulleted list. You can choose from different bullet styles or even use custom images as bullets.

Inserting Images and Graphics

Visual elements like images and graphics can make your presentation more engaging and help explain your ideas visually. Here's how to add them:

1. **Inserting Images**: Go to the "Insert" tab and choose "Pictures". You can insert images stored on your computer or search for images online without leaving PowerPoint. Once inserted, you can click on the image to resize or reposition it according to your slide layout.

2. **Using Graphics**: In addition to standard images, you can enhance your slides with shapes and icons. Click "Shapes" or "Icons" in the "Insert" tab to add these elements. Both options offer a variety of designs to suit any presentation. Shapes are great for creating diagrams or highlighting information, while icons can convey concepts quickly and clearly without using text.

Incorporating SmartArt and Charts

SmartArt and charts are powerful tools in PowerPoint that allow you to represent complex information graphically:

1. **SmartArt**: To insert SmartArt, go to the "Insert" tab and click on "SmartArt". Choose from various categories like Lists, Process, Cycle, Hierarchy, and more. SmartArt is especially useful for creating organisational charts, processes, or even timelines in a visually appealing way.

2. **Charts**: If you need to present data, charts can be extremely helpful. Click on "Chart" in the "Insert" tab, and select the type of chart that best fits your data, such as bar, pie, line, or area charts. PowerPoint integrates with Excel to let you input and edit the chart data directly.

By mastering these basic yet essential skills in PowerPoint, you can create slides that are not only informative but also visually captivating. This foundation will set the stage for more advanced techniques, ensuring your presentations stand out and effectively communicate your ideas.

Managing Slide Transitions

Transitions between slides can enhance your presentation by adding a smooth flow and keeping your audience engaged. Here's how you can manage slide transitions in PowerPoint:

1. **Adding Transitions**: Go to the "Transitions" tab. Here, you'll see a variety of transitions like Fade, Push, Wipe, and more. Click on any transition to preview it on your active slide.

2. **Customizing Transitions**: For each transition, you can adjust the effect options to change how the transition occurs. For example, you might choose the

direction of a Push transition. Additionally, you can modify the duration of the transition to speed it up or slow it down according to your preference.

3. **Applying to All Slides**: If you find a transition you like and want to apply it to all your slides for consistency, click the "Apply To All" button in the Transitions tab. This will ensure that every slide changes with the same transition effect.

Setting Up Slide Animations

Animations are a great way to make your presentation more dynamic and highlight key points. They can be applied to text, images, shapes, and other elements on your slide. Here's how to add animations:

1. **Adding Animations**: Select the element you want to animate, then go to the "Animations" tab. Like transitions, you have a variety of animation styles to choose from, such as Entrance, Emphasis, and Exit effects.

2. **Customising Animations**: After selecting an animation, you can adjust its settings using the options in the Animations tab. This includes the direction of the animation, speed, and whether the animation starts on click, with the previous animation, or after the previous.

3. **Animation Pane**: For more complex animations involving multiple elements, open the "Animation Pane" by clicking its button in the Animations tab. This pane allows you to reorder animations, adjust timings, and fine-tune how animations play during your presentation.

4. **Previewing Animations**: Always preview your animations using the "Preview" button in the Animations tab to ensure they work as expected and enhance the presentation without being distracting.

Reviewing and Finalising Your Presentation

Before you consider your presentation complete, take some time to review and polish your slides:

1. **Spell Check and Review**: Use the "Review" tab to check spelling and grammar. PowerPoint can also provide suggestions for phrasing and concise language.

2. **Rehearse Timings**: Under the "Slide Show" tab, select "Rehearse Timings" to practise your presentation and ensure that your slides align with your planned speaking time.

3. **Slide Sorter View**: Switch to "Slide Sorter View" under the "View" tab to see all your slides at once. This

view is helpful for a final check of slide order and to ensure that all transitions and animations are appropriate.

4. **Feedback**: If possible, present your draft to a friend or colleague to get feedback. Fresh eyes might spot areas that can be improved or point out parts that are unclear.

Exporting and Sharing Your Presentation

Once you've reviewed and finalised your presentation, you'll likely need to share it with others or prepare it for presentation day. PowerPoint offers several options for exporting and sharing your slides, ensuring they can be viewed and accessed in various formats and platforms.

1. **Saving Your Presentation**: Always save your work regularly. Use the "File" tab, select "Save As", and choose the location where you want to save your file. PowerPoint offers different file formats, including the default `.pptx` format. Saving frequently prevents loss of data and ensures you have the latest version of your presentation ready.

2. **Exporting as PDF**: If you need to share your presentation for viewing rather than editing, exporting it

as a PDF is a good option. Go to the "File" tab, select "Export", and choose "Create PDF/XPS Document". This format is widely used because it preserves the layout and formatting of your slides across all devices and platforms.

3. **Creating a Video**: PowerPoint allows you to convert your presentation into a video format, which can be useful for sharing on platforms like YouTube or embedded within websites. In the "File" tab, select "Export", and choose "Create a Video". You can set the timing for each slide and even narrate your presentation to add a personal touch.

4. **Packaging for CD**: If you need to physically distribute your presentation or ensure that it includes all necessary files (like fonts and linked videos), use the "Package Presentation for CD" feature. This option packages your presentation and any associated files into a single folder or CD, making it easy to distribute and run on other computers without compatibility issues.

Preparing for Presentation Day

The final step in creating your PowerPoint presentation is preparing to present it. Here are some tips to ensure you are ready for the big day:

1. **Check Equipment**: Verify in advance that all necessary equipment (projector, laptop, remote clicker, etc.) is available and working properly. Ensure compatibility between your laptop and the presentation equipment.

2. **Practise Your Presentation**: Rehearse your presentation several times. This not only helps you become more familiar with your content but also allows you to manage your timings and transitions smoothly.

3. **Prepare Handouts**: If appropriate, prepare handouts of your slides to distribute to your audience. This can help them follow along and make notes. You can print handouts directly from PowerPoint by going to the "File" tab, selecting "Print", and choosing the "Handouts" option under "Settings".

4. **Arrive Early**: On the day of the presentation, arrive early to set up your equipment and make any necessary adjustments. This gives you time to resolve any unforeseen issues and calm your nerves before the presentation starts.

By following these steps, you'll not only create a strong, engaging presentation but also be well-prepared to deliver it confidently. The skills you've learned in this chapter lay the groundwork for advancing your proficiency with PowerPoint, as we'll explore more complex functionalities and expert techniques in the upcoming chapters.

Chapter 3: Design and Layout

Creating a visually appealing presentation is just as important as the content it contains. This chapter will guide you through using themes, templates, and design tools in PowerPoint to enhance the overall look of your presentation.

Themes and Templates

PowerPoint provides a wide range of built-in themes and templates that can help you achieve a professional look with minimal effort. Here's how to use them effectively:

1. **Selecting a Theme**: A theme includes a set of design elements, including background design, colour scheme, and font styles. To apply a theme, go to the "Design" tab and browse through the theme gallery. Hover over a theme to see a preview of how it will look with your content. Click on the theme to apply it to your entire presentation. If you want the theme to apply only to certain slides, right-click on the theme and choose "Apply to Selected Slides."

2. **Customising Themes**: If you like a theme but want to tweak its appearance, you can customise it. Under

the "Design" tab, click on "Variants", and you'll see options to change colours, fonts, and background styles. This lets you maintain the theme's overall design but tailor it to better suit your specific needs or brand identity.

3. **Using Templates**: Templates are similar to themes but include predefined layouts, content structures, and sometimes sample content. To use a template, when you start a new presentation, choose one from the available templates instead of starting with a blank presentation. This can be particularly helpful if you need ideas for structuring your content.

Customising Backgrounds

A custom background can make your slides stand out and help reinforce the theme of your presentation. Here's how to modify slide backgrounds:

1. **Changing the Background**: To change the background of a slide, go to the "Design" tab and select "Format Background". This opens a pane where you can choose a solid colour, gradient, pattern, or even insert an image as the background. If you want the same background across all slides, click "Apply to All" at the bottom of the pane.

2. **Adding Textures or Patterns**: Instead of a solid colour, you might choose a texture or pattern to add depth to your slides. In the Format Background pane, select "Pattern Fill" or "Picture or Texture Fill" to explore different options that can enhance the visual appeal without distracting from the content.

3. **Keeping It Consistent**: While it's tempting to experiment with different backgrounds, it's important to keep your background consistent throughout the presentation or change it only when transitioning to a new section. Consistency helps keep the audience focused on your message rather than the design changes.

Using these design tools in PowerPoint not only enhances the aesthetic value of your presentation but also makes it more engaging for your audience. By selecting appropriate themes and templates, and customising your slides' backgrounds, you can create a visually coherent and appealing presentation that enhances your message and engages your audience effectively.

Using Master Slides

Master slides are one of the most powerful features in PowerPoint for ensuring consistency throughout your presentation. They allow you to set a default layout and design for various types of slides that you can reuse. Here's how to effectively use master slides:

1. **Accessing Slide Master View**: To start customising your master slides, go to the "View" tab and click on "Slide Master". This will switch your view to a series of slide layouts that make up the master slides for your current theme.

2. **Editing Master Slides**: In the Slide Master view, you can edit the master slide (the top slide in the left pane), which automatically updates all layouts under it, or you can modify individual layouts to address specific needs. For example, you can add a logo, change the footer, or modify background elements that will appear on all slides using that layout.

3. **Creating Custom Layouts**: If the existing layouts don't meet your needs, you can create a new layout by clicking "Insert Layout" in the Slide Master tab. You can add placeholders for text, images, charts, etc., and arrange them as needed. This is particularly useful for creating unique slides that you'll use repeatedly, like section headers or specialised content slides.

4. **Applying Custom Layouts**: Once you've created or modified your layouts, you can apply them to your slides by returning to the normal view (click "Close Master View" in the Slide Master tab). Then, select a slide and go to the "Home" tab, click on "Layout", and choose the layout you've edited or created.

Using master slides effectively can save you a significant amount of time, especially when working on large presentations, and ensures that your slides are uniformly styled.

Alignment and Gridlines

Proper alignment of elements on your slides can make your presentation look more professional. Here's how to use alignment tools and gridlines to lay out your slides neatly:

1. **Enabling Gridlines and Guides**: To help align objects precisely, go to the "View" tab and check "Gridlines" and "Guides". Gridlines give you a grid background to snap objects into place, while guides can be moved and positioned to help align objects as you see fit.

2. **Using the Align Tool**: Select multiple objects by holding down Ctrl and clicking on each object, then go to the "Format" tab, click "Align", and choose from options like Align Left, Align Center, Align Right, Align Top, Align Middle, and Align Bottom. You can also distribute objects evenly by selecting "Distribute Horizontally" or "Distribute Vertically".

3. **Setting Object Positions**: For precise control, you can right-click an object, select "Size and Position", and manually set the position and size. This is useful for ensuring that objects are exactly where you want them, down to the exact measurement.

By mastering these design tools, themes, templates, master slides, alignment, and gridlines you can create a visually stunning and coherent presentation that effectively communicates your message. This foundational knowledge prepares you for more complex design techniques and ensures that your presentations always leave a professional impression.

Chapter 4: Multimedia and Animation

Incorporating multimedia and animation into your PowerPoint presentations can make them more engaging and memorable. This chapter will guide you through the basics of adding audio, video, and animation effects to your slides.

Inserting Audio and Video

Multimedia elements like audio and video can significantly enhance the impact of your presentation when used appropriately. Here's how to add them:

1. **Inserting Audio**:
   - Go to the "Insert" tab and select "Audio".
   - You have two options: you can choose "Audio on My PC" to insert an audio file stored on your computer, or "Record Audio" to record a new audio clip directly within PowerPoint.
   - Once inserted, you can click on the audio icon that appears on the slide to adjust playback options, such as whether the audio should start automatically or on click, and whether it should play across multiple slides.

2. **Inserting Video**:
   - Similarly, go to the "Insert" tab and select "Video".
   - Choose "Video on My PC" to add a video file from your computer, or "Online Video" to insert a video from YouTube or another online source.
   - After adding a video, a set of playback tools will appear under the "Video Tools" tab, allowing you to trim the video, add a fade in and out, and control other settings like volume and whether the video should play full screen.

Both audio and video files can be resized and moved around the slide to fit your layout. It's important to ensure that these multimedia elements support your presentation's message and are not just used as decorative additions.

Animation Effects

Animations can draw attention to key points and make transitions between slides smoother. PowerPoint offers a variety of animation effects that can be applied to text, shapes, images, and other slide elements.

1. **Applying Animations**:
   - Select the element you want to animate and go to the "Animations" tab.

- Browse the gallery of animations "Entrance", "Emphasis", "Exit", and "Motion Paths" are the main categories.
- Click on an animation to apply it to the selected element. Use the "Preview" button to see how the animation will look during the presentation.

2. Customising Animations:
- Once you've chosen an animation, you can customise it further by adjusting its direction, speed, and the order in which it occurs relative to other animations on the slide (Start On Click, Start With Previous, Start After Previous).
- The "Animation Pane" can be opened from the "Animations" tab to manage all animations on the current slide. This pane allows you to reorder animations, tweak timing settings, and more.

3. Advanced Animation Options:
- For more complex animations, explore the "Add Animation" dropdown to combine multiple effects on a single object.
- "Motion Paths" allow you to draw custom paths that elements follow during the animation. This is particularly useful for creating dynamic, eye-catching movements that help illustrate a point or lead the viewer's eye across the slide.

Using multimedia and animations wisely can transform a standard presentation into a dynamic and interactive experience. However, it's crucial to use these tools judiciously so that they enhance the presentation's message rather than detracting from it. In the following sections, we will explore more advanced techniques for using animations and multimedia effectively, ensuring they add value to your presentations.

Action Buttons

Action buttons are interactive elements that can make your PowerPoint presentations more engaging and navigable. They can be used to jump to specific slides, open external files, or link to websites directly from your presentation. Here's how to incorporate action buttons:

1. **Inserting Action Buttons**:
   - Go to the "Insert" tab and select "Shapes". Scroll down to the bottom where you find the Action Buttons, which include symbols like arrows, home, information, and question mark.
   - Draw the action button on your slide. After placing it, a dialog box will automatically appear, prompting you to assign a specific action to the button.

2. **Configuring Actions**:
   - You can configure the button to go to a specific slide, play a sound, or run a custom macro. The most common actions are "Hyperlink to": another slide in the presentation, a different presentation, a document, or an external URL.

- Choose the action that suits your presentation's flow, such as navigating to the first slide, returning to a previously viewed slide, or opening a related document.

3. **Customizing Button Appearance**:
- After inserting an action button, you can customise its appearance like any other shape. Use the "Format" tab to change the fill colour, add effects, and modify the button's text.

4. **Testing Action Buttons**:
- In PowerPoint, you can test the action buttons in "Slide Show" mode. This helps ensure they perform the intended actions and are positioned correctly for easy access during the presentation.

Combining Multimedia with Animations

To create a truly dynamic presentation, consider combining multimedia elements with animations. This approach can help you emphasise points more effectively and keep your audience engaged.

1. **Synchronizing Audio with Slides**:
- You can set an audio clip to play automatically when a slide appears and stop when you transition to the next slide. This is useful for providing narration or background music that is specific to certain parts of your presentation.

- Use the "Playback" tab under "Audio Tools" to set these options, selecting "Start Automatically" and "Stop After Current Slide" for seamless audio integration.

2. **Animating Videos**:
- Apply entrance and exit animations to videos to make them appear and disappear dynamically. For example, a video can slide into the slide from the side and then fade out once it has played.
- These animations are controlled from the "Animations" tab, just like animations for other objects.

3. **Timing Multimedia Elements**:
- The timing of animations and multimedia playback is crucial for a smooth presentation. Use the "Animation Pane" to sequence and synchronise animations with video and audio playback to ensure they activate at just the right moment.
- Adjust the timing settings to delay the start of an animation or to have it occur simultaneously with another animation or action.

By mastering these advanced multimedia and animation techniques, you can create presentations that not only inform but also entertain and engage your audience. Remember, the key to successful use of multimedia and animations is balance; too much can overwhelm your message, but just the right amount can enhance it dramatically. In the next sections, we'll explore further how to use these tools to convey complex information effectively and memorably.

Chapter 5: Advanced Tools and Techniques

In this chapter, we explore some of PowerPoint's advanced features that can help you create more sophisticated presentations. These tools are designed to enhance collaboration, add depth to your data, and streamline your workflow. Even if you're new to these concepts, this section will guide you through each step in a clear and straightforward manner.

Linking and Embedding

Linking and embedding are two powerful ways to include external content in your presentations, whether it's pulling in data from an Excel spreadsheet or incorporating a video.

1. **Linking to External Data**:
   - When you link a file to PowerPoint, it creates a connection to the original file. Any updates made to the original file will be reflected in your presentation.
   - To link an Excel chart, for example, go to the "Insert" tab, choose "Object", then select "Link" and choose the file you want to link. This method ensures that your

presentation data updates automatically as the source Excel file is updated.

2. **Embedding Files**:

- Embedding differs from linking as it incorporates the files directly into your PowerPoint presentation. This means that even without access to the original file, your presentation remains intact with all its data.
- To embed a file, follow the same steps as linking but ensure to select "Embed" instead of "Link". This is particularly useful for ensuring that your presentation is self-contained, making it easier to share across different devices without losing any content.

Both linking and embedding have their uses, depending on your need for real-time data updates or presentation portability.

Collaboration Tools

PowerPoint supports collaboration, allowing multiple people to work on the same presentation simultaneously, which is incredibly useful for team projects and shared presentations.

1. **Using Comments**:

- Comments are a great way to provide feedback without altering the slide content. Click the "Review" tab

and select "New Comment" to add your thoughts or suggestions to a slide.
  - Comments can be targeted at specific parts of a slide, making it easy for reviewers to see exactly what you're referring to and when it was noted.

2. **Co-authoring**:
  - If you're using PowerPoint through Office 365 or SharePoint, you can work on a presentation at the same time as your colleagues. This is called co-authoring.
  - To co-author, simply save your presentation to OneDrive or SharePoint and share it with your team. Everyone with access can open the presentation simultaneously and make changes in real-time.

3. **Tracking Changes**:
  - While PowerPoint does not have a traditional "Track Changes" feature like Word, you can still track revisions by saving versions and using comments. Ensure you regularly save versions to refer back to earlier drafts if needed.

These collaboration tools can drastically reduce the time it takes to prepare a presentation and improve the quality of the final product through diverse inputs and real-time editing.

By leveraging these advanced tools and techniques, you can make your presentations more dynamic, informative, and collaborative. Whether you're managing data with linking and embedding or working with a team through the collaboration features, these capabilities help you take full advantage of PowerPoint's flexibility and power.

Chapter 6: Efficiency and Expert Tips

Now that you've learned the basics and some advanced techniques, it's time to focus on making your work more efficient. This chapter is packed with tips, shortcuts, and expert advice to help you create and edit presentations faster and with greater precision.

Keyboard Shortcuts

Using keyboard shortcuts can significantly speed up your workflow in PowerPoint. Here are some essential shortcuts that will make your life easier:

1. **Basic Shortcuts**:
    - **Ctrl + N**: Create a new presentation.
    - **Ctrl + O**: Open an existing presentation.
    - **Ctrl + S**: Save the current presentation.
    - **Ctrl + P**: Print the presentation.
    - **Ctrl + Z**: Undo the last action.
    - **Ctrl + Y**: Redo the last undone action.

2. **Editing Shortcuts**:
    - **Ctrl + X**: Cut the selected item.

- **Ctrl + C**: Copy the selected item.
- **Ctrl + V**: Paste the copied or cut item.
- **Ctrl + A**: Select all items on the slide.
- **Ctrl + B**: Bold selected text.
- **Ctrl + I**: Italicise selected text.
- **Ctrl + U**: Underline selected text.

3. **Slide Navigation**:
- **F5**: Start the presentation from the beginning.
- **Shift + F5**: Start the presentation from the current slide.
- **Esc**: Exit the presentation mode.
- **Page Up/Page Down**: Move to the previous or next slide.

4. **Formatting Shortcuts**:
- **Ctrl + M**: Insert a new slide.
- **Ctrl + D**: Duplicate the selected slide.
- **Ctrl + Shift + Up/Down Arrow**: Move a slide up or down in the slide order.
- **Ctrl + G**: Group selected objects.
- **Ctrl + Shift + G**: Ungroup selected objects.

Slide Master Advanced Use

We've touched on using the Slide Master to ensure consistency, but there are advanced ways to leverage this feature to save even more time and enhance your presentations.

1. **Creating Custom Layouts**:
   - In the Slide Master view, you can create entirely new layouts that can be reused throughout your presentation. This is particularly useful for complex presentations with varied content types.
   - To do this, click "Insert Layout" in the Slide Master view, then customise it with text boxes, images, and placeholders as needed.

2. **Using Placeholder Text and Images**:
   - Placeholders can be customised to indicate where specific types of content should go. This helps maintain a consistent look and feel, even when different team members are adding content.
   - Insert placeholders for text, pictures, charts, and more by going to the "Slide Master" tab and selecting "Insert Placeholder".

3. **Global Changes**:
   - If you need to make a change that applies to all slides, such as updating the font style or adding a logo, you can do it in the Slide Master. These changes will automatically apply to every slide that uses the affected layouts.
   - This saves time and ensures uniformity across your presentation.

Tips and Tricks

Here are some expert tips to take your PowerPoint skills to the next level:

1. **Use the Presenter View**:
   - The Presenter View is a powerful tool that allows you to see your notes, the current slide, and the next slide all at once, while your audience only sees the current slide.
   - To enable it, go to the "Slide Show" tab and check the "Use Presenter View" box. This can help you stay on track and deliver your presentation more smoothly.

2. **Customising the Ribbon**:
   - You can customise the ribbon to include the tools you use most frequently. Right-click on the ribbon and select "Customise the Ribbon" to add or remove commands.
   - This customization can streamline your workflow and make your favourite tools more accessible.

3. **Quick Access Toolbar**:
   - The Quick Access Toolbar is a great place to store your most-used commands for easy access. You can add items to it by right-clicking any command in the ribbon and selecting "Add to Quick Access Toolbar".

4. **Using Sections**:
   - For large presentations, use sections to organise your slides. Right-click between slides in the thumbnail

pane and select "Add Section". This helps manage complex presentations and allows you to collapse or expand sections as needed.

5. **Embedding Fonts**:
   - To ensure your presentation looks the same on any computer, embed the fonts you use. Go to "File > Options > Save" and check "Embed fonts in the file".
   - This prevents issues with missing fonts when presenting on a different device.

By incorporating these efficiency tips and shortcuts into your workflow, you can create high-quality presentations more quickly and with less effort. These techniques not only save time but also help you produce more polished and professional results. In the final chapter, we will discuss how to prepare and deliver your presentation with confidence, ensuring you make a lasting impression.

Chapter 7: Preparing for Presentation Day

You've put in the work to create a compelling, well-designed PowerPoint presentation. Now it's time to make sure everything goes smoothly on the day you present. This chapter will guide you through the final steps of preparation, practice tips, and techniques for delivering a confident, engaging presentation.

Review and Proofing Tools

Before presenting, it's crucial to review and proof your slides to ensure they are error-free and polished.

1. **Spell Check and Proofreading**:
   - Go to the "Review" tab and click on "Spelling" to run a spell check on your presentation. PowerPoint will highlight any spelling errors and suggest corrections.
   - Proofread your slides manually to catch any grammar issues or awkward phrasing that the spell checker might miss. Reading your slides out loud can help you notice mistakes.

2. **Use the Thesaurus**:

- If you find yourself using the same words repeatedly, use PowerPoint's thesaurus feature. Highlight a word, right-click, and select "Synonyms" to find alternatives.

3. **Check for Consistency**:
   - Ensure that fonts, colours, and styles are consistent across all slides. This creates a professional and cohesive look. Use the "Slide Master" to make any necessary global changes.
   - Verify that all images and graphics are aligned properly and that there are no overlapping or misaligned elements.

Practice Tips

Practising your presentation is key to delivering it smoothly and confidently. Here are some tips to help you prepare effectively:

1. **Rehearse with a Timer**:
   - Use PowerPoint's "Rehearse Timings" feature to practise your presentation with a timer. Go to the "Slide Show" tab and click "Rehearse Timings". This will help you gauge how long your presentation takes and adjust your pacing if necessary.

2. **Use Presenter View**:
   - Practice using the "Presenter View" to become familiar with seeing your notes, current slide, and

upcoming slide all at once. This view helps you stay on track and remember key points without needing to glance at your printed notes.

3. **Record Your Practice Sessions**:
   - Record yourself practising your presentation. Watch the recording to identify areas where you can improve your delivery, such as speaking too quickly, using filler words, or failing to make eye contact with your audience.

4. **Simulate the Presentation Environment**:
   - Practice in a setting similar to where you'll be presenting. If possible, use the same equipment and setup to become comfortable with the technology and space.

5. **Seek Feedback**:
   - Present your slides to a friend or colleague and ask for constructive feedback. They might notice issues or have suggestions that you hadn't considered.

Presenting Like a Pro

On the day of your presentation, these tips will help you deliver with confidence and professionalism:

1. **Arrive Early**:

- Arrive at the presentation venue early to set up your equipment and ensure everything is working properly. This gives you time to troubleshoot any issues and reduces pre-presentation stress.

2. **Check Your Equipment**:
   - Test your laptop, projector, remote clicker, and any other equipment you'll be using. Ensure your slides display correctly and that any embedded multimedia works smoothly.

3. **Stay Calm and Confident**:
   - Take deep breaths and stay calm. Confidence comes from preparation, so trust in the work you've done to create and practise your presentation.

4. **Engage with Your Audience**:
   - Make eye contact with different parts of the audience, and use natural gestures to emphasise points. Engaging with your audience helps keep their attention and makes your presentation more memorable.

5. **Handle Questions Gracefully**:
   - Be prepared for questions from the audience. Listen carefully, repeat the question if necessary, and provide thoughtful answers. If you don't know the answer, it's okay to say you'll follow up after the presentation.

6. **Use Visual Aids Effectively**:

- Rely on your slides as visual aids rather than reading from them verbatim. Your slides should complement your spoken words, not replace them.

7. **Have a Backup Plan**:
   - Always have a backup plan in case something goes wrong. Bring printed handouts, a backup copy of your presentation on a USB drive, and be ready to present without multimedia if necessary.

By following these preparation and presentation tips, you'll be well-equipped to deliver a successful and impactful presentation. Confidence, practice, and attention to detail will ensure that your hard work pays off and that you make a lasting impression on your audience.

Conclusion

Congratulations on mastering the art of creating and delivering PowerPoint presentations! This book has taken you from the basics to advanced techniques, empowering you with the skills needed to craft professional, engaging presentations. Remember, the key to success is practice and continuous improvement. Keep experimenting with new features and techniques, and soon you'll be a PowerPoint pro.

Thank you for choosing Skipton Tech's guide to mastering Microsoft PowerPoint. We hope this book has been a valuable resource on your journey to presentation excellence. Happy presenting!